W9-DFH-982

PAPERCUTTING

To my late Uncle Hugo
and to my husband Michael

1 A Chinese luck hanging

PAPERCUTTING

Brigitte Stoddart

Taplinger Publishing Company
New York

First published in the United States in
1973 by
TAPLINGER PUBLISHING CO., INC.
New York, New York

Library of Congress Catalog Card Number:
72-5302
ISBN 0-8008-6247-3

Contents

Acknowledgment

Figures 5, 10, 11 and 12 are from
Beseelte Schatten and reproduced by
kind permission of the publishers
Buchheim Verlag, Munich.

Unless otherwise stated, all the
illustrations are by the author.

2

Introduction

Papercutting has never been regarded as a great art form. Its champions have created cuts for pure pleasure and their appeal is for decoration today, discard and replace tomorrow. The ephemeral quality is reflected in their flimsy structure and like that of a flower or a snowflake, their beauty although short-lived is nonetheless real.

3

What is papercutting?

At its simplest, a paper cut can be a stylised flower shape cut out of paper and pasted onto a background of contrasting colour. At its most complex it can be a large multicoloured panel involving layer upon layer of tiny slivers of paper, each separately shaped and then carefully assembled to make an integral picture. Alternatively, it may be a single cut, so intricate as to involve all the techniques possible with scissors and knife.

The following pages show how anyone can create his or her own flat paper decorations, and how they can be used in a multitude of ways. Here is a chance to experiment in something creative, unusual and, above all, personal.

There is nothing difficult about papercutting – indeed it is as simple as cutting paper. Anyone can make cheap and effective cuts with most rewarding results, and, as with all skills, experience doubles the reward.

Historical Notes

4 A composition with a bird, a snake and two butterflies, 10 in.×11 in. (240 mm×279 mm), by Amelia Blackburn   *British Museum*

An old German manuscript puts forward the belief that England was the first European country to adopt the art of papercutting. If this is so we have no evidence for it, as the first recorded cuts were made in the late seventeenth century, some thirty years after the first cuts were recorded in Germany.

However, there is sufficient material to show that for two hundred years papercutting was a positive art in England, springing mainly from the work of Mrs Delaney and then later from that of Miss Amelia Blackburn. Their papercut pictures had a style all of their own, in which many different shades of coloured paper were applied and the picture was built up from small slivers rather than being cut out of one large piece. Birds, flowers and wreaths were the most popular topics, all dealt with in a realistic way, creating, as far as possible, an exact likeness to the original. Amelia Blackburn's work was the more artistic and became so popular that for a long time papercuts were referred to as 'Amelias'. See figure 4.

The Victorians really took to papercutting and practised it at the fireside along with embroidery and tapestry canvas work. At about the same time Valentine cards with lacy paper motifs became fashionable and were used extensively all over England.

Facing page
6 A portrait of the artist's children cut in 1828 by August Edouart

5 An eighteenth century lacework Valentine motif from Germany

Although papercutting began in England at about the same time as in Germany or Poland it has not been kept up in the same way as in these two countries. Polish cuts have always been gaily coloured and stylised floral designs or circular black 'doilies'. They were made to decorate the home and would be taken down and replaced at intervals, probably because the paper used was dyed with vegetable dyes, which fade badly. Nowadays cuts are still used in this way, but they are also widely made for a tourist market.

7

8

12

9

7, 8 and 9 The author's painted
impression of three Polish cuts from the
Horniman Museum

In Germany early cuts were white on black and strangely enough colour was never used. The effect was later reversed to black on white, which still remains traditional. All kinds of rural scenes were depicted and even now German cuts tend to be realistic rather than stylised. Originals are rarely seen, but they are printed widely onto cards and calendars and are used for book illustrations.

10 to 12 Nineteenth century German cuts by unknown artists

10 The tools and symbols of martyrdom

Facing page
11 The trial of a hunter by the animals. This reflects the fact that hunters probably started the craft in Germany and this cut was possibly made by the hunter himself while in a satirical mood about his eventual fate

15

12 A rural scene. Note the disregard for
perspective which is characteristic of
such cuts

13 The author's painted impression of a
typical eighteenth century cut from
Germany or Austria

Another type of cut is seen in Mexico where the craft has flourished since the invention of paper. Here the cuts, delicate filigree designs of birds and flowers on tissue paper, were used in interment ceremonies and were usually destroyed in the process. It was thought that a cut buried with the body had the power of ushering the spirit to eternity.

Similar burial rites were performed in China. The dead were supposed to receive an estate in Hades equal to the number of paper effigies of worldly goods, money, cattle, servants, etc that were buried alongside them. Here again the papercuts were destroyed almost as soon as they had been made. Besides this papercuts were and still are widely used to decorate homes. They are referred to as 'luck hangings' and serve to ward off evil spirits which may enter the home. Similar cuts are used in Indo China and the figures on page 26 are from Vietnam.

Figures 14 to 18 are from China and show a range of animal and fish motifs of which 14 and 15 were doubtless designed for their grace and beauty as well as for any supposed power they may hold. It is normal for cuts used for this purpose to be renewed frequently. The same traditional designs occur again and again, with slight variations. Perhaps traditional evil spirits are fought with traditional weapons!

14

15

14 to 18 Chinese luck hangings

16

19

18

The theatre figures, facing page 16, are typical, traditional designs from the Ho-Pei province. Many designs are multicoloured, but red is a favourite colour for the plain cuts and black is seldom used. For generations there have been professional papercutters in China who have modified the designs to reflect changing conditions. Modern cuts show the progress of the country and depict agricultural scenes, laboratory research and factory life.

It is inconceivable that designs in paper have not been made in almost every country of the world, but it is only in Germany, Poland, Mexico and China that this craft has reached international fame.

19

19–22 Modern cuts from China

21

24

23 Modern cuts from Vietnam

Tools and Materials

Very little equipment is needed for papercutting. Preliminary experiments may be made with ordinary household scissors and an old paper bag. However, if the cuts are to be mounted a better quality paper will be necessary and I recommend gummed paper for simpler cuts and plain paper of the same quality for more complex work. The reason for this is that the layer of gum tends to add thickness to the paper, but it also makes the fingers sticky when one piece of paper is handled for any length of time.

For best results the requirements are as follows:

The smallest and most pointed scissors available (some embroidery scissors are suitable, but dissecting scissors are ideal)

A packet of assorted gummed paper

A packet of assorted plain paper

Exacto knife

Paste

Compass

27

Simple and Basic Cuts

An easy exercise, reminiscent of the chains of dolls and Christmas trees that we all made as children, is perhaps the best approach to the art of papercutting.

Something along the lines of figures 24 and 25 can be made by anybody (these were made by five-year-olds) in a very few minutes.

Fold thin paper (tissue or kitchen paper) into quarters, sixths or eighths (or in a zigzag) and cut out bold, distinct shapes from all the folded edges. This is quick, effective and fun and an impression can be gained of the possibilities that this art form holds.

Closed silhouettes

Simpler, but not so striking are closed silhouettes which are described first as they are the most basic form of this craft. They have no internal detail but rely

24

entirely on the outline for effect. For this
reason it is advisable to choose a motif
with an interesting and characteristic
shape. Ideas can be found in children's
picture books, which show stylised forms
of flowers and animals.

The motif may stand on its own, but
can often be made to look more
attractive by the addition of grass or
flowers underfoot. Figures 26, 27 and 30.

The design should be drawn on the
back of the paper, first in full, including
internal lines, then making a heavier
pencil line along the cutting edge. A
gold rule to remember is that every
cutting line should join up with its own
beginning. The more complex the cut, the
more difficult it becomes to see at a glance
that this rule has been kept and it is
always advisable to check before cutting.

Time and effort may be saved by cutting
the most complicated parts first. There are
two good reasons for this:

1 that these parts are the easiest to spoil
and that, if they are spoilt, the whole
cut may as well be started again
straight away

2 that it is easier to cut these difficult
parts from a whole shape than from
one which is already floppy, delicately
formed and may easily tear.

For many closed silhouettes this may
not apply, but it is a useful point to be
remembered as progress is made. Figure 34
was begun by cutting out the detail, the
main outlines were left until last.

25

26

Avoiding tearing

When cutting round the motif it becomes increasingly difficult to avoid tearing, because the scissors get tangled with the surround, which has already been cut away. Often this situation can be helped by cutting off the unwanted parts at intervals. See figure 28.

28

27

Approaching a corner

A right-hand bend should always be approached from underneath and a left-hand bend from above (figure 29). This is very important as the cuts become more complicated: if the rule is not observed the arms of the scissors will catch and bend or even tear parts that have already been cut. Moreover, if the cut is kept as flat as possible throughout, further accidental tearing can often be avoided.

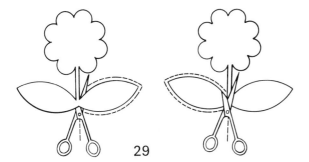

29

30

31

Framing

When the cut has been made it is fun to experiment with different colours of background or to mount it with a frame of the same colour. See figures 32 and 111.

31

32

◄ A panel comprising simple but effective
cuts each mounted on coloured paper
with small pieces of colour inserted and
stuck over

33

34

Folded Closed Silhouettes

35

These are made in the same way as plain silhouettes except that the paper is first folded lengthways, and the design is consequently duplicated. Where the central motif is symmetrical and only half of it is drawn against the fold it is often useful to open out the paper and first draw the motif on both sides of the fold in order to make it the correct width (refold before cutting). Flower motifs, trees or human figures especially need this treatment. Figures 35, 37 and 41 were all made in this way, but 36, 39 and 42 were drawn straight onto the folded paper. Where the motif cannot be symmetrical it can be drawn just touching the fold so that the cut still hangs together when opened out, but has no central motif (figure 38). In order to keep the two layers of paper together while cutting it is usually best to begin at the edge and work towards the fold.

36

37

38

39

35

Figure 40 is a copy of a traditional Polish cut, which has been made in the same way as other cuts in this section, though it is much bolder in style.

40

41

Four-folded closed silhouettes

For these, flower motifs or just simple shapes are most suitable as people or animals look odd upside-down! With four-folded cuts it is more important than ever to cut the delicate parts first. It so easily happens that the four layers separate and shift slightly as progress is made. Figures 43 and 44 are examples of four-folded silhouettes without outer frames. Figure 43 has a central panel which was cut away first and then cut separately. It is not in silhouette like the remainder but has a design in white on black.

Framing closed silhouettes

Any symmetrical shape of frame may be obtained by trimming the raw edges after folding and before drawing the design. Figures 45 and 46 show how a square or rectangle can be used. Figure 48 shows a circle which had been folded into six parts, and figure 47 was cut from a triangle which had been folded into eight parts. Naturally it is not so easy to cut through eight layers of paper at once, therefore it is wise to use a simple design for such cuts and rely on the repetition for effect. Figure 49 was first folded into four, then the open edges were trimmed before the design was drawn.

Where a papercut has a joined frame the design should be carefully spaced to avoid any large unfilled gaps. Unless the cut is very small it is also important for the motif to be joined to the frame or to itself (at connecting points) as frequently as possible. This avoids too great a degree of flimsiness.

44

45

46

47 Triangle folded into eight parts

48 Circle folded into six parts

49 Circle folded into four parts and the
open edges trimmed before the design was drawn

42

Some Simple Techniques

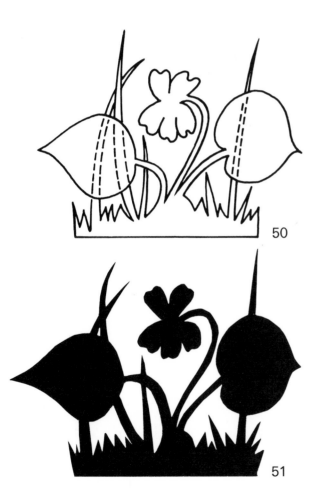

50

51

Internal spaces

Whenever it is necessary to make a hole as a starting point for cutting out an internal space it is best not to use the points of the scissors unless the part to be cut out is very large. It is surprising how easily a small slip of the scissors can spoil the work. The cut should be placed on several layers of newspaper and the initial incision made with an *Exacto* knife (or guarded razor blade) pressed down firmly. This is clean, neat and quite safe.

Overlapping

With silhouettes these internal spaces can only occur where shapes overlap or just touch one another (figure 50). Make sure that overlapping shapes are fully drawn first so that a long blade of grass, for instance, does remain quite straight although it is partially covered by a leaf (figure 51).

43

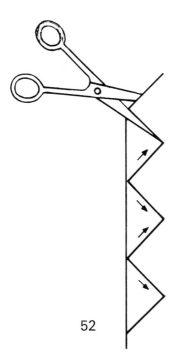

Connecting points

These occur wherever two motifs touch or where the motif touches the frame. They are useful for holding together a large cut and preventing it from becoming floppy.

Zigzagging

For a large zigzag it is easy enough to follow the cutting line with the scissors, turning them this way and that to negotiate the corners. For a finer zigzag, however, it may be much easier to cut all the points with the scissors facing into the cut (figure 52). Use the very ends of the scissor blades and judge as exactly as possible how much blade to use; it is then safe to snip right to the points without fear of cutting off the previous zigzag.

52

Silhouettes with Coloured Slivers Added

Once the silhouette is made there are all sorts of possibilities in the realm of colour, mounting or framing; smaller motifs cut out of coloured paper may be added, so changing the whole style of the cut.

The colour plate facing page 33 shows how nine relatively simple cuts were mounted on coloured paper and had small pieces of colour inserted or stuck over.

Clashing colours can often give a stunning but not unpleasant effect. It is impossible to give a satisfactory impression of this in black and grey, but a very simple experiment may be made by cutting out the black part of figure 53 in dark red, the single flower shape in bright pink, the first pair of leaves in orange and the second in purple. The whole is then mounted on a piece of blue or turquoise paper and framed in orange or yellow. A small child would be capable of working

53

out this or a similar design. Figures 54 and
55 both show silhouettes that have had
some colour added.

Many Polish cuts are made by cutting a
central black or dark green motif and then
adding the individually cut flowers and
leaves afterwards. One flower can be
composed of four or five layers of
differently coloured paper and the artist is
able to move about the various motifs
until he finds a satisfactory composition.
Once again, this (and similar papercutting
methods) is a very rewarding pastime for a
child, as each piece can be safely put
down while the next is worked. Figures
56, 57 and 58 were all made in this way,
though figure 58 was worked out entirely
in black, grey and white, while the other
two are multicoloured.

54

55

56—58 Papercuts in Polish style

47

57

58

48

Open Silhouettes

59

In the old tradition of German papercutting the 'open' cut was regarded as being an infringement of the rules, but for many years now 'open' cuts have been made and accepted in that country. They are an interesting and inevitable advance on the plain silhouette.

The open silhouette is simply a papercut involving cuts to depict internal detail; in fact, it is no longer a true silhouette, but rather a representation in cut paper. It may be realistic or stylised and almost any picture or motif may be translated into this medium with the help of the internal cut to overcome the problem of formlessness and bulk.

The Chinese papercutters have never been silhouette-minded and among their open cuts are some very attractive and intricate designs. As well as scissors the Chinese papercutters use specially shaped knives and gouges to form the internal details. These tools are pressed straight down onto the paper, and in this way many cuts can be made at once, especially as a particularly thin variety of paper is used. Many Chinese designs are traditional as is the *Boy with Apple* (figure 60).

60

Although it is very effective it is, in fact, very easy to cut out. All the little circles and leaf-shapes are tedious with scissors, but no trouble when made with the special tools.

The colour plate facing page 16 shows traditional Chinese theatre figures, which are made by professional papercutters.

Sixty or seventy layers of thin paper are tacked down onto a frame and all cut together. The paper is then dyed the various colours by placing droplets of the dye solution on the top paper and allowing it to soak through. It is said that the bottom papercut turns out as perfect as the top one.

61

Paper Doilies

62 Circle folded into sixteen parts

Doilies are quick and simple to make while they appear to be complex. This is because it is possible to fold the tissue paper that they are made from into sixteen parts and still have detailed designs. Only a very few cuts are then needed to obtain the filigree effect. Tissue paper is so thin that it is difficult to flatten out the completed cut, but by ironing it with a very cool iron through a sheet of thin paper this problem can be overcome.

Figure 65 was cut in the Polish style and was folded into thirty-two parts. Often this type of Polish cut has small slivers of colour added.

63 Circle folded into eight parts

54

◀ 64 Circle folded into sixteen parts

65 Circle folded into thirty two parts

66 Circle folded into
thirty two parts

56

Folded Open Cuts

67

68

While paper doilies only involve cutting small shapes out of a plain background so that the small shapes form the design, the folded open cut can be approached in a variety of ways.

Figure 69 is almost a folded silhouette except for the internal detail on the figures, but figure 67 is much nearer the style of a doily, though it is only folded into four, which allows for the much bolder central design.

Figure 68 shows well the importance of connecting points; the two hearts and two leaves were intentionally cut separately.

The more complex the cut the greater is the tendency for it to become flimsy and figures 70 and 71, though intricate, are far from frail, as they have an abundance of connecting points. Figure 71 was only folded once so that it was possible to achieve greater detail.

69

70

71

73

60

72

74

75

76

77

61

Figures 78 and 79 are both cut in the same style. Much of the traditional Polish and German work looks like this. The floral shapes are very stylised and worked out with a compass, then the very smallest holes are cut out first. Papercuts like these are very suitable for any kind of greetings card.

78

79

Techniques for Open Silhouettes

By using a knife or wood-engraver's gouge various patterns and textured effects can be obtained. Most of these methods are suitable only for a single layer of paper.

Chequer-boarding

This technique can be used to depict basket-work, roof tiles, floor tiles or fabric. It is very important to draw out the design accurately and then cut each shape slightly smaller than drawn (figure 80). This part of the cut should be made first and it is wise to begin by practising on scrap paper. Figure 81 shows how this technique has been used to add perspective to the picture, and in figure 82 it represents the fabric of the witch's apron.

80

63

Dots, dashes, small shapes

There is no quick way of making these when they occur in an otherwise complex cut. Each must be cut separately with knife or scissors. Scissors are better where curves are involved and an *Exacto* knife (not drawn, but pressed straight down) can be used for any straight edges. The witch's house in figure 82 shows some of the shapes that can be cut. Figure 83 has tiny floral shapes representing the design in the girl's dress. It also has chequerboarding for her basket.

81

A complex open cut transformed by
the addition of coloured slivers

82

83

Striping

This is fairly straightforward and just needs special care. If the stripes to be cut are no longer than 25 mm (1 in.) they may be cut with a sharp knife, but if they are to be longer it is usually easier to start with a knife and continue with scissors. Figures 84 and 85 show uses of striping.

84

85

86

Circling

This effect is achieved by cutting a series of incomplete circles, each joined to the next at a different point (figure 87). Scissors are best for this, though the initial cut should be made with a knife. A similar effect can be obtained by folding the paper into quarters and cutting as in figure 86. This can form the outside of a cut (figure 88) or the centre (figure 89).

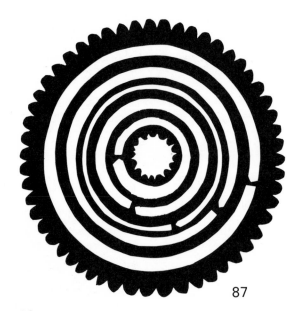

87

88

89

90

Open silhouettes with colour inserts

Once an open flower motif has been cut it is fun to experiment with colour inserts, and in its simplest form this method will appeal to children. Often it is interesting to make two identical cuts and only insert colour in one. Figure 91 is the plain cut corresponding with the colour plate facing page 65 which has the inserts. The Chinese exploit this type of cut and they often use gold paper for the 'outline'.

Figure 92 is an example of a four-folded cut with colour inserts. Figure 90 has only been folded once, and has only a minimum of inserts all in grey.

91

92

▶

Quite a different type of motif is shown in figure 93, which has inserts of various colours; the windows were added last of all.

93

Cuts incorporating one other colour

Figure 95 is an open silhouette with a frame as part of the cut. It is shown here on a grey background, though it is also effective on white.

Figure 94 comprises a black cut and a grey cut. The two were designed to fit together and six of the flower shapes were cut separately and assembled with the rest.

94

95

Random Folding

Instead of always folding the paper into exact quarters or eighths it can be fun to make three or four random folds and cut a design through all the thicknesses. Some results of this are shown in figures 96 to 103. It will be noticed that many of these cuts appear to have been folded in half, but this was not the case; the first fold just happens to have become central as the cut was made.

96

97

98

99

100

101

102

103

Picture~Making with Several Layers of Cuts

Another way of using papercutting techniques is to make several cuts (in different shades or even in contrasting colours) that fit neatly over one another to make one integrated picture. The success of this depends upon accurately tracing the finished picture onto every paper and then picking out, with a heavier pencil line, the parts to be represented on each individually. Another way of doing this is to build up the picture by first cutting the 'background' colour (a), then laying it onto the next colour (b), drawing round the cut edge of (a) and deciding which parts to cut the same as (a) and which parts to leave that were cut away in (a). Having cut (b) the same procedure is followed for (c) until the picture is finished. Figure 104 and the colour plate facing page 81 are examples of such cuts, while figures 105 and 106 show earlier stages in cutting.

104

105

106

Several layers of cuts fitting neatly over
one another to make an integrated picture. ▶

80

Assembling Cuts

Where the cuts are to be used as a wall decoration it can be attractive to put several together to form one large panel. The colour plate facing page 33 is an example of such an assembly. The nine cuts were all made from the same size of paper so that they would fit exactly together. There are many possibilities with this type of cut: the assembled panel may be any required shape and as large or as small as desired. All the component cuts could, for instance, be triangles, diamonds, floral shapes or rectangles. A variety of shapes could be incorporated in one assembly, or just two that fit well together (figure 107). Figure 108 shows an assembly of rectangles and squares; some are duplicated, others are not; some are black on white, others white on black. Each cut is relatively simple to make on its own, but when the whole is assembled

107

the effect is one of complexity. This is fun
to make and arrange and very suitable for
children to try out. A more complex
assembly is shown in figure 109, which has
four identical shapes that have all been cut
differently, and, in the centre, a specially
shaped cut with the design in reverse, ie
white on black.

108

109

Mounting Cuts

It is important always to have clean hands when mounting and to deal with one section at a time. The glue should be carefully applied to the centre first so that the cut can be positioned, then the remainder can be gently raised, and the glue applied to those parts large enough to support a small blob without it coming over the edge. Finally, any delicate parts that are in danger of getting crumpled or bent back can be stuck by raising them with tweezers and applying the glue with the tip of a kitchen knife.

110

Uses for Cuts

Apart from wall decorations, framed pictures and wall panels cuts can be used to decorate such things as lampshades, furniture, gift boxes, cigarette boxes, for cards and calendars or to decorate any kind of rack or rail. They can be stuck with thin *Polycell* and be thrown away and renewed when they become 'dog-eared', or for 'permanence' they can be sealed with polyurethane.

For greetings cards all kinds of motifs are suitable and can be quickly made by children or adults. In figures 110 to 121 a selection of suitable motifs can be seen. Some are designed for specific occasions, while others would be useful for a variety of purposes. Abstract patterns are often just as effective as actual representations, and figures 122 to 125 are four-folded cuts made by young children.

111

A child's nursery can look delightful with a large assembled cut pasted straight onto the wall. As children grow older they can make their own wall decorations.

113

112

114

115

116

117

88

118

119

120

121

89

122

124

123

125

126

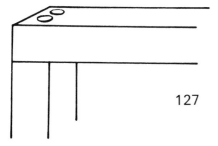

127

How to use cuts to make simple prints

Materials

4 pieces of soft wood 203 mm × 25 mm
× 25 mm (8 in. × 1 in. × 1 in.)
8 panel pins
Stapler and staples or staple gun
Roll of 25 mm (1 in.) wide brown sticky
paper
Kitchen paper (a coated medium weight paper)
Newspaper
A pair of men's rubber shoe heels that
have one straight edge, or one squeegee
in the smallest size available
Organdie – about 46 cm ($\frac{1}{2}$ yard)
Fabric dye for printing

Making the screen

Make a square frame by nailing the four
pieces of wood together.
Sand down rough edges so that the
frame will lie flat on a table. Cut a square
of organdie about 254 mm × 254 mm
(10 in. × 10 in.) and lay it under the
frame. The organdie should then be folded
at the edges and stapled one side at a
time onto the top of the frame so that it is
taut underneath. Next turn the frame over
so that the organdie is on top and proceed
to 'mask' all but a central square of about
76 mm to 102 mm (3 in. to 4 in.) of the
frame by sticking successive strips of
brown paper onto the organdie and
overlapping it at the edges. Continue to
stick strips of brown paper over the frame,
over the staples and right into the inside,
until the organdie has been masked to the
same point both inside and out. The screen
is now ready to be used.

128

129

Printing

Mix the dye in a separate jar, adding water until it has a consistency similar to that of treacle. Cut the design out of kitchen paper, beginning with a piece slightly larger than the square left unmasked on the screen. Mark a square on the paper slightly smaller than that on the screen and cut the design within this limit. When cutting it should be remembered that all parts cut away will show in the print while the rest will remain the colour of the paper or fabric to be printed upon.

The design should then be laid onto a piece of paper which, in turn, is on several layers of newspaper. The screen is laid onto the design (with the organdie at the bottom) so that the design is exactly in the middle. Place about two teaspoonsful of dye on the brown paper along one inside edge of the screen and then draw it over the design with the squeegee (or shoe heel) pressing it firmly. When printing on fabric the squeegee should be drawn over several times, but this is not necessary on paper. When the screen is lifted the design will remain on the underside and if several prints are required they should be made without delay, as the dye easily clogs up the organdie. It should be possible to make about twenty prints before the design begins to disintegrate. If more prints are required several identical cuts can be made at the outset and used in succession.

Figures 128, 129 and 130 are prints suitable for Christmas cards. Figure 130 shows the design cut out in black above and the printed version underneath. Figures 131 and 132 were printed onto fabric.

Overleaf
131 A cut paper design used as a silk screen resist and printed in brown on yellow fabric

132 A silk screen print, made in the same way, glued onto heavy card to make a book cover

130

Suppliers

GREAT BRITAIN

Papers

All kinds from

Paperchase
216 Tottenham Court Road
London W1

Dryad Limited
Northgates, Leicester
also screen printing equipment

F G Kettle
127 High Holborn
London WC1

Many art shops stock assorted squares of gummed back paper but the range of colours is often limited.

Dissecting scissors

Buck and Ryan
101 Tottenham Court Road
London W1

and from most hardware shops and department stores.

USA

Different kinds of papers obtainable from art stores, stationers and department stores, also direct from

The Morilla Company Inc
43 21st Street, Long Island City
New York and 2866 West 7th Street
Los Angeles, California

Stafford-Reeves Inc
626 Greenwich Street
New York, NY 10014

Winsor and Newton Inc
55 Winsor Drive
Secaucus, New Jersey 07094

Squeegees and screen printing equipment

Silk Screen Suppliers Inc
32 Lafayette Avenue New York, NY

Card   Thin white cardboard
Polycell   Wallpaper paste
Gummed back paper   coloured paper
  adhesive backed.